9|3|13
$8.99
dP
JRef

Regions of the United States: The Southeast

Jennifer Blizin Gillis

Raintree

Chicago, Illinois

Produced for Raintree by
White-Thomson Publishing Ltd,
Bridgewater Business Centre,
210 High Street, Lewes, BN7 2NH

Page layout by Malcolm Walker
Photo research by Amy Sparks
Illustrations by John Fleck
Printed and bound in the United States of America, North Mankato, MN

15 14 13
10 9 8 7 6 5

**Library of Congress
Cataloging-in-Publication Data**

Gillis, Jennifer Blizin, 1950-
  The Southeast / Jennifer Blizin Gillis.
     p. cm. -- (Regions of the USA)
  Includes bibliographical references and index.
  ISBN 1-4109-2308-8 (hc) -- ISBN 978-1-4109-2316-5 (pb)
  1. Southern States--Juvenile literature. I. Title. II. Series.
  F209.3.G55 2007
  975--dc22

                          2006004814
062013
007422RP

Acknowledgments
The publisher would like to thank the following for permission to reproduce photographs:
pp. 4, 16–17 Tom Till; p. 5, 24, 26, 27A, 29B, 35B Gibson Stock Photography; p. 6 David Fraizer; p. 8 Corbis/ Raymond
Gehman; p. 19 I-stock/Dan Brandenberg; pp. 29A, 51A Bill Russ/NC Division of Tourism, Film and Sports Development;
pp. 9, 27B, 30, 33, 38, 41, 42, 47, 49, 51B Jeff Greenburg; p. 10 Philip Gould/CORBIS; pp. 11 National Parks Service;
pp. 13, 31 Topfoto; pp. 14A, 21B, 23, 25, 32, 37, 46 Viesti; p. 15 Cezary Gesikowski/I-stock; p. 18 UPPA/Photoshot;
p. 20 OSF/Photolibrary; p. 21A I-stock/John Richbourg; p. 22 James Randklev/CORBIS; p. 28 Teake Zuidema/The
Image Works/Topfoto; p. 34 Lester Lefkowitz/CORBIS; 35A The Image Works/Topfoto/David Fraizer; p. 36
www.ci.kannapolis.nc.us; p. 39 PIERRE DUCHARME/Reuters/Corbis; p. 40 The Image Works/Topfoto; p. 43
OSF/Photolibrary/Foodpix; p. 44A Reuters/CORBIS; p. 44B Steve Boyle/NewSport/Corbis; p. 45 Jon Gardiner/Icon
SMI/Corbis; p. 48 I-stock/Doug Webb; p. 50 Gene Burch

Cover photo of Florida Everglades reproduced with permission of photolibrary.com

Contents

The Southeast 4

People and History 8

Land in the Area 14

Animals and Plants 20

Cities and Towns 24

Rural Life 30

Getting Around 34

Work in the Area 36

Free Time 40

An Amazing Region 50

Find Out More 52

Timeline 53

States at a Glance 54

Glossary 55

Index 56

Some words are shown in bold, **like this.** You can find out what they mean by looking in the glossary.

The Southeast

If you flew over the Southeast region of the United States, you would see a wide range of landscapes. Beaches along the southern and eastern coasts lead to fields of crops, then dense forests of pine and **hardwoods** farther inland.

Rolling hills toward the west lead to mountains, where some of the highest peaks on the East Coast are located in the Appalachian Mountains. You would also find friendly people. Many of these people live in the Southeast because of its history, **climate**, and landscape, or for the jobs available in this region.

Y'all come!

Southern hospitality is world famous. In sprawling **metropolitan** areas and sleepy small towns alike, visitors get a warm welcome. Perhaps it's because of the summer heat, but people in the Southeast take time to "sit a spell" with neighbors or drink a glass of sweet tea with friends. "Y'all come" is an old-fashioned southern expression that means "Everyone is welcome."

A clearing sky reveals a row of ridges along the Blue Ridge Parkway in the Appalachian Mountains.
▼

4

Fun in the sun

Tourists come here year-round for different reasons. Winter tourists can soak up the sun on a south Florida beach or sled the snow-covered hills of Tennessee. Fall visitors to the mountains of North Carolina, Georgia, and Arkansas can admire the brilliantly colored leaves.

Other visitors to this area might come for spring festivals— from Saint Patrick's Day in Savannah, Georgia, to Mardi Gras in New Orleans, Louisiana. Others come for summer hiking along the Appalachian Trail or a cooler walk below the ground in Mammoth Cave, Kentucky.

Seven states in the Southeast have beaches on the Atlantic Ocean or the Gulf of Mexico, so water sports are popular in the Southeast.

▼

Find out later...

Where can you find champion racehorses grazing in fields?

How many bedrooms does this famous estate have?

What are these people celebrating?

5

In the Sunbelt

The Southeast is in a part of the United States known as the Sunbelt because of its warm climate, and sunny weather. Low taxes, inexpensive homes, and an expanding **economy**, in addition to the pleasant climate, help make the Southeast one of the country's fastest-growing regions.

A diverse culture and a rich, colonial history also largely define this region. Unique offerings such as Mardi Gras celebrations in New Orleans and **Dixieland music** are two traditions that draw many people to the region, either as visitors or permanent residents.

Sunny Outlook

The Sunbelt boasts some of the warmest weather in the United States. More than half the days in a typical year are sunny in cities such as Jackson in Mississippi, Nashville in Tennessee, and Raleigh in North Carolina. In Columbia, South Carolina, 64 of every 100 days are sunny.

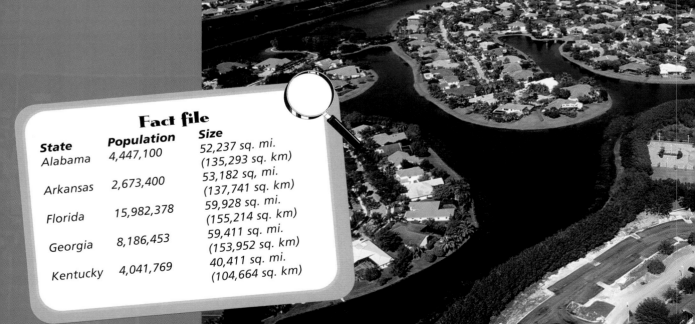

As more people move to the Southeast, open land near cities such as Miami has given way to densely packed housing developments. ▼

Fact file

State	Population	Size
Alabama	4,447,100	52,237 sq. mi. (135,293 sq. km)
Arkansas	2,673,400	53,182 sq, mi. (137,741 sq. km)
Florida	15,982,378	59,928 sq. mi. (155,214 sq. km)
Georgia	8,186,453	59,411 sq. mi. (153,952 sq. km)
Kentucky	4,041,769	40,411 sq. mi. (104,664 sq. km)

A region of change

The Southeast has been through many changes. Once, farming was the region's biggest business. Today, companies that produce everything from cars to prescription drugs bring workers from around the world.

Once, the region was known for its small towns. Today, spreading metropolitan areas and **mass transit** systems connect more people and places. Large metropolitan areas in the region include Charlotte in North Carolina, Atlanta in Georgia, and Nashville and Memphis in Tennessee. In Florida, the biggest cities are Jacksonville, Orlando, Tampa/St. Petersburg, and Miami. These cities are among the 50 most populated cities in the United States.

Fact file

State	Population	Size
Louisiana	4,468,976	49,651 sq. mi. (128,595 sq. km)
Mississippi	2,844,658	48,434 sq. mi. (125,444 sq. km)
North Carolina	8,049,313	52,672 sq. mi. (136,421 sq. km)
South Carolina	4,012,012	32,008 sq. mi. (82,901 sq. km)
Tennessee	5,689,283	42,143 sq. mi. (109,150 sq. km)

People and History

The mild temperatures and great resources of the Southeast have attracted **immigrants** for centuries. Native Americans were the first people to live in the Southeast. Native American groups such as the Cherokees, Choctaws, Chickasaws, Creeks, and Seminoles all lived in this region.

As European settlers began to arrive in the 1600s, they forced these Native Americans from their land. Today, less than one percent of the population of the Southeast is Native American. The Cherokee nation, with a total population of 369,035, is the largest tribe in the United States, although only a small group remains in the Southeast.

The Trail of Tears

In 1838 the U.S. government forced more than 15,000 Cherokees to leave Georgia, Kentucky, Tennessee, and North Carolina. They were marched to territory that later became Oklahoma. Many did not survive the march, which became known as the Trail of Tears. The Trail of Tears National Historic Trail was later created to remember the removal of the Cherokee from their lands. This system of national parks is spread over 2,200 square miles (5,698 square kilometers) across nine states.

Osceola (1804-1838) was the leader of the Seminoles in Florida. He is wearing a traditional outfit made from animal skins.

European settlers

The coastal areas of the Southeast were first settled in the early 1600s. Explorers claimed large blocks of land across the region for Spain, France, and England. Settlers from these countries as well as Scotland, Ireland, and Wales established colonies.

Some Europeans brought slaves from Africa and the Caribbean to work on their huge farms. Other Europeans came to the Southeast as craftspeople and servants. Many who live in the Southeast today are **descendants** of these original settlers and slaves.

Saint Augustine, Florida, the first lasting European settlement in what became the United States, was founded by the Spanish in 1565.

▼

The lost colony

In 1584 Queen Elizabeth I of England asked Sir Walter Raleigh to colonize America. A year later, 100 British citizens arrived on Roanoke island off the coast of present-day North Carolina to start a colony. Within two years, most of the colonists returned to England due to a shortage of supplies and hostile relations with nearby Native Americans. Although fifteen colonists stayed behind, a new group of colonists that arrived in 1587 found no sign of the earlier group. Historians have been trying to solve the mystery of the "lost colony" ever since.

Cajuns and kilts

The Spanish were the first Europeans to discover the Mississippi River, but the French started the first settlements there. In 1682 they named the area around the mouth of the river Louisiana in honor of King Louis XIV of France, who was the king of France at the time. The United States made the **Louisiana Purchase** from France in 1803. This land included the states that would later become known as Louisiana, Mississippi, and Arkansas.

Today, many people living farther inland from the Southeast coasts are descendants of settlers from Great Britain, Ireland, and Germany. People from Scotland settled in the mountains of North Carolina, Tennessee, and Georgia.

Cajuns

In the 1700s French settlers were forced from the colony of Acadia, in what is now Canada. They joined a small group of French settlers who had been living in Louisiana. Over time, they mixed with the local population, which included Native Americans, African Americans, and people from Germany and Spain. The word *Cajun* evolved from the British pronunciation of the word *Acadians*. The Cajun language is a rich mix of French, German, Spanish, and Native American words.

Cajun music combines accordions, guitars, and fiddles with unusual instruments such as washboards played with finger picks.
▼

The struggle for independence

During the **Revolutionary War,** wealthy planters in coastal areas mostly stayed loyal to Great Britain because their continued wealth and power depended on a good relationship with the king. Settlers living farther inland sided with the **patriots.**

Several important Revolutionary War battles were fought in the Southeast. The **Continental Army** defeated the British at the Battle of Kings Mountain in South Carolina in 1780. The following year, colonists defeated the British at the Battle of Cowpens before heading north toward Virginia. The British caught up with the colonists in North Carolina, but they had lost so many soldiers that they surrendered in 1783.

This monument commemorates the Revolutionary War battle fought at Cowpens, South Carolina.

▼

The Edenton tea party

On October 25, 1774, women in the seaport town of Edenton, North Carolina, passed a resolution not to drink tea or wear clothes made in Great Britain. This action encouraged patriots in Boston, who had worried that wealthy southerners would not support their struggle for independence.

The Civil War

In the 1800s the wealth of the coastal Southeast came from an economy based on slavery. Many people in northern states had wanted to outlaw slavery during the Revolutionary War. But powerful southern lawmakers always prevented antislavery laws from passing.

Abraham Lincoln, who was against slavery, was elected president of the United States in 1860. At that time South Carolina, the wealthiest southern state, separated from the United States. Ten other states followed soon after. Kentucky was the only state in the Southeast not to join the new government of the Southern states, the **Confederate States of America.**

The Confederate States of America

The Confederate States were not well prepared for war. Basic items, such as weapons, shoes, and food, were in short supply. The states did not cooperate with each other, either. Some states that had enough supplies refused to share with other states. On April 9, 1865, General Robert E. Lee surrendered the Confederate army to General Ulysses S. Grant at Appomattox Courthouse, Virginia. Each Confederate state had to apply to be allowed back into the **Union**.

Slow recovery

After the Civil War, slavery was outlawed. Poor blacks and whites became **sharecroppers**, farming small plots of land and paying rent with the crops they grew. Many of these people lived in poverty.

Civil rights

White southerners were angry when African-American men got the right to vote after the Civil War. Southeastern states passed laws that made African Americans pass difficult tests before they could vote. Other laws made it illegal for African Americans to mix with whites at restaurants, schools, or theaters. In 1964 the U.S. government struck down these laws, but it took many years to bring equal rights to parts of the Southeast.

Cotton mills

Following the Civil War, the Southeast became the nation's top producer of **textiles**. Cheap land, large supplies of cotton, and workers who accepted low pay and bad working conditions brought factory owners to the region. Textile mills were the region's largest employers until late in the 1900s, when companies shifted their operations overseas because it was cheaper for them to produce products there. The region still produces about 60 percent of the cotton in the United States, but most clothing is no longer made here.

◄ Dr. Martin Luther King Jr., center, leads a group of civil rights supporters on a march to Selma, Alabama, in the 1960s.

13

Land in the Area

The Cape Hatteras Lighthouse in North Carolina had to be moved to a new location so it wouldn't be washed away. ▼

Beaches are among the most outstanding land features of the Southeast. North Carolina, South Carolina, Georgia, and Florida have coastline bordering the Atlantic Ocean. Florida also has coastline bordering the Gulf of Mexico, as do Alabama, Mississippi, and Louisiana. The land that borders the Gulf of Mexico is known as the Gulf Coast.

Many people live near beaches and on the **coastal plain** in the Southeast. As more people have moved to the region, **wetlands** and **swamps** have been drained so that houses can be built. There has also been a bigger demand for land and water. This demand means more water has been drained and this has weakened the land. As a result some low spots are actually sinking.

Shrinking and sinking

Many beaches along the Atlantic Coast of the Southeast are threatened by **beach erosion**. Barrier islands are small islands that stop ocean waves before they crash on the shore of the **mainland**. Waves from the Atlantic Ocean have washed away barrier islands that once protected the mainland beaches.

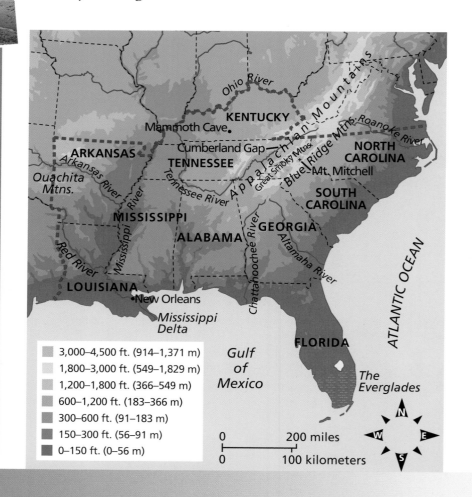

Ohio River

KENTUCKY
Mammoth Cave.

Cumberland Gap

ARKANSAS
Arkansas River
Ouachita Mtns.
TENNESSEE
Tennessee River

Appalachian Mountains
Great Smoky Mtns.
Blue Ridge Mtns.
Roanoke River

NORTH CAROLINA
Mt. Mitchell

SOUTH CAROLINA

MISSISSIPPI
ALABAMA
Mississippi River
Red River
GEORGIA
Chattahoochee River
Altamaha River

LOUISIANA
•New Orleans
Mississippi Delta

Gulf of Mexico

FLORIDA

ATLANTIC OCEAN

The Everglades

▨	3,000–4,500 ft. (914–1,371 m)
▨	1,800–3,000 ft. (549–1,829 m)
▨	1,200–1,800 ft. (366–549 m)
▨	600–1,200 ft. (183–366 m)
▨	300–600 ft. (91–183 m)
▨	150–300 ft. (56–91 m)
▨	0–150 ft. (0–56 m)

0   200 miles
0   100 kilometers

N
W   E
S

Coastal plain

Just inland from the beaches is coastal plain. The low, flat ground of the coastal plain may often be flooded, and swamps and **bayous** dot the region. A bayou is a slow moving stream or creek, usually located in low-lying areas, such as the Mississippi **Delta**. In fact, the French in Louisiana were the first to use the word *bayou* to describe this landform.

An environmentalist and writer named Marjorie Stoneman Douglass wrote a book about the Everglades. She called the Everglades "a river of grass."

▼

Most of the Southeast's **cash crops**, such as peanuts, cotton, tobacco, sugar, fruit, and soybeans, grow in the light, sandy soil of the coastal plain.

The Florida Everglades

The largest subtropical wetlands in the United States is Everglades National Park. It covers more than 1.5 million acres (607,050 hectares) in southern Florida. Fifteen of the park's plant and animal species, such as the Florida panther, the American crocodile, the green turtle, the West Indian manatee, and the Cape Sable seaside sparrow, are **endangered**. One of the biggest threats to plants and animals is Florida's growing population, which has led to the increased draining of water from the Everglades.

Piedmont

Farther inland from the beaches, slightly rolling hills and thicker plant life are characteristic of the **piedmont**, or foothills. Arkansas, Alabama, Georgia, Kentucky, North and South Carolina, and Tennessee have piedmont regions. This is where Scottish, Irish, English, and German immigrants established small settlements and farms.

Forests

Most of the Southeast is heavily forested. The pines of the coastal plain give way to hardwood forests of the mountains. Trees such as oak, hickory, and ash have made the region a major producer of furniture. Pines are used in the production of paper products and building materials.

Going west

Daniel Boone (1734–1820) is a famous U.S. pioneer. Drawings often show him wearing buckskin clothing and a hat made from the fur of a raccoon. He did not have a formal education, but he was an experienced outdoorsman by the age of 12. In 1769, he helped explore the Cumberland Gap, a route across the Appalachian Mountains into Kentucky. Later, he helped blaze "the Wilderness Road" from North Carolina to Kentucky, where he started a settlement named Boonesborough with a party of 30 settlers.

Beginning in the late 1700s, many pioneers passed through what is today the Cumberland Pass National Park in Kentucky.

Mountains

Half of the Southeast region's ten states include mountains. The Appalachian Mountain chain extends into North Carolina, South Carolina, Kentucky, Georgia, and Alabama. Along its eastern edge lie the Blue Ridge Mountains, which are so named because of their misty blue color.

The Great Smoky Mountains of Tennessee are among the oldest mountain ranges on Earth. Farther west the Boston Mountains in northern Arkansas are the highest part of the Ozark range. The Ouachita Mountains run from east to west, from central Arkansas to Oklahoma.

Fact file
At 6,684 feet (2,037 meters), Mount Mitchell in North Carolina is the highest peak in the Southeast.

Mammoth Cave

Mammoth Cave in south central Kentucky is the world's longest known cave system. More than 360 miles (580 kilometers) of the underground system has been explored and mapped. Even so, there is still more to be discovered under the ground there. Mammoth Cave National Park offers different tours within the cave system.

Ice storms

Snow is not a typical part of winter throughout much of the Southeast. Icy rain, however, regularly falls, coating streets and plants. Although beautiful, this kind of storm can be dangerous. The weight of the ice can bring down power lines and tree limbs. Each winter, crews work day and night to bring electricity back to areas where ice storms have caused power outages.

Weather and climate

The Southeast region is a big area with a range of different climates. The mild climate for which the Southeast is best known occurs as a result of humid, **tropical** air from the Atlantic Ocean and the Gulf of Mexico. Humidity, the amount of moisture in the air, can make a July day in parts of the Southeast feel like a steam bath!

Mild temperatures keep winters fairly warm on the coast and in the coastal plain, though snow is not uncommon in the piedmont and mountains of Georgia, North Carolina, and Tennessee, and in parts of Kentucky.

Snow often coats the tree limbs on a Kentucky mountainside in the winter.
▼

Hurricanes

Hurricane season in the Southeast lasts roughly from early June to the end of November, with most hurricanes occurring in September. The warm waters of the Gulf of Mexico and the Atlantic Ocean feed these powerful storms, which brew in the ocean before hitting land.

In 2005 the Gulf Coast was battered by Hurricane Katrina, which came to shore with winds of more than 155 miles (249 kilometers) per hour. In New Orleans, one of the lowest points in the United States, the hurricane left up to 75 percent of the city underwater.

Hundreds of people died and whole communities were flooded during Hurricane Katrina in 2005.

Destructive molds

Though mold can live anywhere, it is especially a problem in buildings soaked by major storms. One type of mold, called "black mold," feeds on building materials, such as paint, drywall, wood, and fabric. If not treated in time, it can ruin buildings. Following Hurricanes Katrina and Rita in 2005, libraries in Alabama, Louisiana, and Mississippi lost books, computers, and even buildings to mold.

Animals and Plants

The wildlife of the Southeast is as varied as its landforms. The region's animals range from crabs along the Gulf and Atlantic coasts to black bears in the mountains, and everything in between. The Southeast is home to oak and magnolia trees, and a climbing vine called kudzu.

Coastal wildlife

Coastal wildlife includes large fish such as sailfishes, marlins, dolphins, and rays. Birds such as pelicans, seagulls, sandpipers, ospreys, blue herons, and egrets are a common sight on both the Atlantic and Gulf coasts.

Sea turtle rescue

Green sea and loggerhead turtles are endangered animals native to the waters of the Atlantic Coast. Green sea turtles can weigh as much as 440 pounds (200 kilograms) and build nests only on the Atlantic Coast of Florida. Loggerhead sea turtles can weigh as much as 200 pounds (91 kilograms). They build nests on open beaches on both the Atlantic and Gulf Coasts.

Scientists track the movements of loggerhead turtles.

Wetlands animals

The wetlands and swamps of the Southeast region are full of wildlife. Lizards, salamanders, toads, frogs, turtles, and snakes live among the roots of cypress trees. Wading birds such as blue herons, bitterns, and egrets fish the dark waters. Bald eagles, owls, and red-tailed hawks feed on small reptiles, rodents, and rabbits.

In the bayou

The bayou of the Mississippi delta is home to many types of fish. Crawfish, certain types of shrimp and other shellfish, and catfish thrive here.

The ruby-throated hummingbird beats its wings 40 to 80 times each second. ▶

Alligators are native to the swamps of the Southeast. ▼

Ruby-throated hummingbirds

Hummingbirds sip nectar from plants in gardens throughout the Southeast from late spring until early fall, when most begin their winter journeys to Mexico. Because they weigh just a few grams and move so quickly, they may be mistaken for bugs.

Garden paradise

Much of the Southeast's climate is **subtropical**. It is not unusual to see tropical plants such as palm trees or hibiscus growing in gardens alongside daisies and lilies. The region's growing season is longer than that of northern areas, so two crops of vegetables can be harvested between Memorial Day and late October.

Grapefruits, oranges, and lemons grow in Florida's tropical areas. In fact, with 97 million fruit trees, Florida is the world leader in grapefruit production. Only Brazil produces more oranges than Florida.

Bald cypress trees

Bald cypress trees are native trees of the low, swampy land of the coastal Southeast. Bald cypress trees were once a major part of the economy of the Southeast. They were plentiful, they did not rot easily, and the wood was easy to work with. In the early 1900s, logging operations nearly wiped out the bald cypress tree. But now the trees are seen again across the region.

The bald cypress is Louisiana's state tree. ◄

22

Creepers and climbers

Just like people who move south for the mild climate, some plants have made the Southeast their home. In fact, some **invasive plants** grow better in the Southeast than they did in their native areas.

Some people call kudzu the mile-a-minute plant because it can grow up to 1 foot (.3 meters) a day during warm weather. In the 1930s, government workers planted kudzu throughout the Southeast to hold soil in place and keep it from washing away. By the 1970s, when kudzu was declared a weed, this Japanese bean vine covered acres of trees, buildings, and telephone poles.

Southeast trees

Pines are the most common trees in the heavily forested Southeast. Hardwoods such as oak, ash, and maple grow in the piedmont and mountains.

Kudzu grows so thickly that it blocks out light, killing the trees and plants that it covers.

Cities and Towns

In the past there were few truly big cities in the Southeast. Most cities grew up before the Civil War around ports or railroad junctions. Their wealth came from sales of crops such as cotton or tobacco.

The economy of the Southeast was crushed during the Great Depression of the 1930s. As businesses closed and jobs became scarce, people moved away from Southeast cities to cities such as Chicago and New York City to try to find new jobs. By the 1970s the downtowns of many cities in the Southeast had few stores or restaurants. They were deserted at nights and on weekends.

Urban sprawl and Atlanta

Urban **sprawl** happens when the suburbs outside cities grow bigger than the cities themselves. Shopping centers, office parks, and houses take the place of farms, fields, and forests. Some cities in the Southeast take up huge amounts of land. For example, the metropolitan area of Atlanta, Georgia covers 1,963 square miles (5,084 square kilometers).

Atlanta, Georgia, is one of the most sprawling metropolitan areas in the world.

▼

Southern revival

These days, skyscrapers are a common sight across the Southeast. Charlotte, North Carolina, is a good example of this rebirth. The city was established in 1755. Soldiers in the Continental and British armies camped here during the Revolutionary War. The U.S. government opened a branch of the U.S. **Mint** in Charlotte in the mid-1800s. The city stayed wealthy, even after the Civil War, but it remained small. In the late 1970s, two local banks began buying up banks around the country. They became giant companies that brought many workers to the area, creating a need for more houses, stores, restaurants, and other services.

Charlotte, North Carolina, has grown into a major banking center. It is the headquarters of Bank of America and Wachovia, two of the largest banking companies in the United States.

Big cities

The largest city by population in the Southeast is Jacksonville, Florida, with just over 773,000 people. Memphis, Tennessee follows with a population of 645,978 and then Charlotte, North Carolina with 584,658 people. These population statistics, however, do not take into account the entire metropolitan area. For example, Atlanta itself has 423,000 people, but its metropolitan area has a population of nearly 5 million people!

St. Augustine

The Spanish explorer Juan Ponce de León discovered and named present-day Florida as he was searching for the legendary Fountain of Youth. He established a colony at St. Augustine in 1513. The Spanish, French, and British fought over the city, and it changed hands many times before it finally became part of the United States after the Revolutionary War. Today, the narrow streets, tiled roofs, courtyards, and walled gardens of the old city remind tourists of its long history.

Coastal towns

Europeans began settling the coast of the Southeast in the 1500s and 1600s. As the colonies grew, some of the original settlements became busy seaports or colonial capitals, such as New Orleans. A French explorer founded New Orleans at the mouth of the Mississippi River on the Gulf Coast in 1718. The city passed back and forth between French and Spanish hands until the early 1800s, when France sold it to the United States as part of the Louisiana Purchase.

Bits of Spanish, Caribbean, African, and French heritage have had a lasting effect on the people, architecture, music, and food of New Orleans.

◄ Lace-like wrought iron balconies in the French Quarter of New Orleans show its Spanish and French heritage.

Miami's mixture

Spanish explorers first visited the land around Miami, Florida, in the 1500s. Until the late 1800s, only the Seminole tribe and descendants of early Spanish settlers lived in the area. The railroad opened the area for development, and the population grew from 1,500 people in 1900 to nearly 30,000 in 1920. Today, Miami's metropolitan area has a population of about 5 million.

Miami has a large Hispanic population. Between 1960 and 1990, hundreds of thousands of immigrants from Cuba and Haiti flocked to the city. Miami is the third largest port for immigration after New York City and Los Angeles. Miami is also home to large groups of immigrants from Israel, Russia, Finland, and France.

Houses in the heart of Savannah, Georgia, are built on squares filled with flowers and trees.

Miami's location on the Atlantic Coast helps to draw many visitors to nearby beaches.

Savannah, Georgia

In the 1700s General James Oglethorpe and 120 British colonists started a settlement on land near the Savannah River. Oglethorpe designed Savannah with wide streets and many public squares. It was the first planned city in the colonies. During the Civil War, Union General William Sherman burned nearly everything in Georgia between Atlanta and the Atlantic Ocean except the beautiful city of Savannah.

Located on the Mississippi River, Memphis was named after an Egyptian city on the Nile River. Memphis is world famous for its musical heritage, which includes blues, rock and roll, and gospel. Elvis Presley, "the King of Rock and Roll," recorded at Sun Studio in Memphis. Aretha Franklin, Tina Turner, Johnny Cash, and blues great B. B. King all started out in Memphis.

Sun Studio music recording studio opened in Memphis, Tennessee in the 1950s.

Heading west

Spanish and French explorers traveled through parts of what became Arkansas, Kentucky, Mississippi, and Tennessee in the 1500s and 1600s. But few Europeans moved to these areas until the 1700s. This was because it was difficult for early settlers to cross the Appalachian Mountains. Pioneer and explorer Daniel Boone opened the way for others when he blazed a trail across the Appalachians into Kentucky in the late 1700s.

Many "western towns" of the Southeast began as forts or places to trade goods with Native Americans. A French explorer started the town of Little Rock, now the capital of Arkansas, as a trading post.

Resort towns

Some towns grew up around natural features, such as hot springs, and became famous as health resorts. Wealthy people from the North built vacation homes in these places, and towns grew up around the services and businesses that catered to these visitors. At the end of the 1800s, wealthy factory owners were building summer homes in the Appalachian Mountains. Later, in the 1920s, several Florida towns became fashionable winter resorts. Florida remains a popular destination for northerners escaping cold winters.

People bathed in the natural hot springs at Warm Springs, Georgia, to improve their health. President Franklin D. Roosevelt was a frequent visitor. He stayed in this house, called "The Little White House."

Biltmore Estate

More than 100 years ago a wealthy railroad owner, George Vanderbilt, set out to build America's largest home as a retreat for friends and family. After six years of construction, his summer home in Asheville, North Carolina (above) was completed in 1895. Visitors may tour the mansion's 250 rooms (including more than 30 bedrooms), indoor pool, bowling alley, and gardens, but overnight stays are not allowed.

Rural Life

Farming is at the heart of the Southeast. Though small numbers of people in the Southeast make their living by farming and most small farmers have other jobs, large-scale farming is still an important part of the economy.

Many people in the region live on farms that were established by their parents or grandparents. Though more transportation means that rural areas are not as difficult to get to as they once were, farm families often have to drive long distances to shop or get medical help.

Small towns

The Southeast is as well known for its sleepy towns as it is for its sprawling metropolitan areas. Driving through the countryside on back roads, there are many communities that have one or two businesses, a few houses, and perhaps a church. These are settlements that grew up to serve the farms around them. As fewer people make their living from farming, many of these small communities have been abandoned.

Sweet corn is one of the many crops that grow well in Southeastern states such as Florida.

The Deep South

Some of the poorest people in the United States live in parts of the Appalachian Mountains and the Deep South. The Deep South is an area that includes the states of Alabama, Arkansas, Georgia, and Mississippi. In rural areas, some people live in poverty in run-down houses without indoor plumbing or electricity. In the past few years, organizations such as Habitat for Humanity and the Rural Agricultural Advancement Foundation have worked to improve living conditions for people living in rural communities in the Deep South.

Hobby farms

Some people move to the Southeast because farmland is still available there. They may start "hobby farms," on which they raise a few animals and grow some crops to feed their families or for fun.

Small, family farms in the Southeast raise a variety of crops. Farmers often sell extra produce such as vegetables, melons, and peaches at open-air markets.

Until the middle of the 1900s, cotton was the most important cash crop of the Southeast. It is still an important crop. While Texas now grows the most cotton in the United States, Alabama, Arkansas, Georgia, Louisiana, Mississippi, North and South Carolina, and Tennessee are still major cotton-producing states.

The way things were

Tobacco was once one of the most important crops in the Southeast. The lives of many communities were organized around the tobacco crop cycle. In many counties the school year did not start until after the tobacco crop had been harvested. With the drop in tobacco use, farmers in the Southeast have had to grow new crops. Some states have tobacco buyouts, meaning they pay tobacco farmers a certain amount of money based on the amount of tobacco the farmers used to raise and sell.

Fact file

The state of Georgia is the top peanut producer in the United States. Alabama, North Carolina, and Florida rank third, fourth, and fifth in peanut production.

In the late 1940s, more than 500,000 tobacco farms operated in the United States. The number had dropped to 57,000 by the year 2002.

Factory versus free range

Hogs and poultry are among the most important livestock raised in the Southeast. Most of these animals are raised on "factory farms." In factory farming, one company raises the animals, prepares the meat, and packages it for sale. Factory farm animals live in long metal houses and often receive special foods and medicines that keep them healthy or make them grow larger.

For people who prefer to eat foods without added drugs or chemicals, other farmers raise "free-range products." These are meats and eggs that come from animals that are not given drugs or chemicals and who spend their days outside eating grass.

Going organic

Many farmers who used to raise cotton, tobacco, or other crops are now turning to organic farming. In organic farming, crops are raised without chemicals, such as fertilizers or **pesticides**. Such chemicals protect crops but may be harmful to people or the earth.

This farmer is feeding calves on a dairy farm in Alabama. ▼

Getting Around

MARTA

The Metropolitan Atlanta Rapid Transit Authority (MARTA) began as a bus system in the 1950s. In the 1960s MARTA began planning for a **light rail** system that would connect the five counties around Atlanta with the city center. Tracks were laid and stations were built over the next 25 years. By 2000 the system had carried more than 3.5 million passengers.

Since agriculture for many years was the most important industry in the Southeast, the region needed a good system of roads so farmers could get their crops to market. Dusty, red-dirt roads far out in the country and one-lane bridges still exist, however.

The growth in population in the Southeast has caused many problems with roads. Heavier traffic has caused local roads to wear out faster. Construction to widen narrow roads slows traffic. When bad weather forces people to leave parts of the Southeast, cars get trapped in huge traffic jams on roads that were built for far less traffic.

Large urban areas in the Southeast such as Atlanta can experience heavy traffic congestion.
▼

Ports

With borders on the Atlantic Ocean and the Gulf of Mexico, the Southeast has many important ports. The Port of New Orleans is one of the largest cargo ports in the United States. Products such as steel, coffee, and forest goods pass through the port on their way into or out of the United States.

Cargo also passes through the Port of Miami, but Miami is more famous as the world's largest cruise ship port. It is the home port of nearly twenty cruise ships. Three million passengers a year take cruises that leave from this busy seaport.

Barges and freighters like this one are a common sight on the Mississippi River.

The Tennessee-Tombigbee Waterway

The "Tenn-Tom" is a 234-mile (376-kilometer) canal that connects river ports in the Southeast with the Gulf of Mexico. It begins at the Tennessee River in northeastern Mississippi and ends at the Black Warrior and Tombigbee rivers in central Alabama.

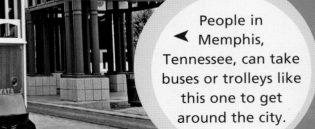

People in Memphis, Tennessee, can take buses or trolleys like this one to get around the city.

Work in the Area

Fishy business

Aquaculture—fish and alligator farming—is big business in the Southeast. More than 400 farms in the Mississippi Delta raise 75 percent of the nation's catfish and provide more than 4,000 jobs. About 200,000 pounds of alligator meat are harvested from Florida alligator farms each year.

Most jobs in the Southeast today are in manufacturing, food processing, and the **service industry**. These industries have replaced the textile and tobacco industries as the region's biggest employers. The biggest retailer in the world, Wal-Mart, got its start in Arkansas in the 1960s. Today, Wal-Mart has almost 5,000 stores around the world and employs more than 1 million people.

Textiles

Textile mills were built in the Southeast from the late 1800s until the 1930s to process the cotton crops grown there. Because most mill workers came from distant rural communities, business owners often built **company towns**, with houses, stores, and churches just for the workers. In many places medium-sized cities have grown out of company towns.

The Pillowtex textile factory in Kannapolis, North Carolina, closed in 2003. Kannapolis is one example of a company town in the Southeast.
▼

Feeding the United States

Food processing is a major industry in the region. Arkansas-based Tyson Foods leads the nation in raising chickens and making them into food products. Tyson also produces pork and beef products. The company has more than 80 plants that employ more than 120,000 workers.

Southern-fried businesses

Several popular fast foods got their start in the Southeast. Krispy Kreme doughnuts started in Winston-Salem, North Carolina, in 1937. Kentucky Fried Chicken (KFC) got its start in 1939, when the colonel Harland Sanders began selling his tasty fried chicken. Today, KFC employs more than 250,000 people worldwide.

Fact file

One of every three steaks sold in the United States is produced by Tyson Foods.

The world-famous bottle

Coca-Cola was invented by an Atlanta pharmacist in 1886. Within twelve years, it was being sold all over the United States and in Canada and Mexico. Today, Coca-Cola brands include juices and bottled water.

The Coca-Cola Museum in Atlanta, Georgia, tells the history of the famous soft drink.

Many universities in the Southeast, such as Duke University in Durham, North Carolina, are also home to major medical centers. In 2005 nearly 233,000 people in North Carolina had health care jobs, and Duke University was the third-largest employer in the state.

Tourism

Because the Southeast has beaches and mountains that draw many people to the region, the tourist industry is a major employer here. Hotels, restaurants, tour boats, tour buses, campgrounds, cruise ships, amusement parks, gardens, and zoos provide thousands of jobs in the region.

The Southeast's rich history also provides jobs for many people. Guides conduct walking tours of historic towns such as St. Augustine, Florida, and New Orleans, Louisiana. Some guides may show how people lived in the past by acting as though they live in times past at historic farms, plantations, and parks.

Florida theme parks are popular attractions for tourists from around the world.

Fact file

Florida is the number-one travel destination in the world. The state has more than 370,000 hotel rooms and 700 campgrounds. In 2004 nearly 77 million tourists visited the state.

Jobs in science and space

There are jobs for scientists and engineers throughout the southeastern states. The Oak Ridge National Laboratory in Tennessee, the U.S. Army's missile research center in Alabama, and the National Aeronautics and Space Administration (NASA) Marshall Space Flight Center, also in Alabama, all provide thousands of jobs. The Kennedy Space Center in Cape Canaveral, Florida, is another major employer.

Petroleum industry

Far out in the Gulf of Mexico, oil companies drill for petroleum and natural gas. Barges, boats, and helicopters move people and products to and from the platforms in the Gulf. Oil production in the Gulf of Mexico was interrupted by Hurricane Katrina in 2005. The disruption caused high gas prices all over the United States.

The U.S. space program has brought many jobs to cities in the Southeast, such as Cape Canaveral, Florida, home of NASA's space shuttle.

Fact file

Huntsville, Alabama, is known as Rocket City USA because of the research and space flight centers there.

Free Time

Preservation Hall

Close to the Mississippi River, in the French Quarter of New Orleans, Preservation Hall has stood since the mid-1700s. Home to several businesses over the years, Preservation Hall became a music hall featuring New Orleans jazz in 1961.

The rich mix of people in the Southeast has affected the region's music. In fact, the region is sometimes called the Cradle of American Music. Here, the rhythms and culture of the Caribbean, Africa, the United Kingdom, and France blended into musical styles that are uniquely American. Bluegrass, blues, and jazz music were born here. Country and rock-and-roll have strong ties here, too.

Nashville, Tennessee, is famous for its music. In fact, it is nicknamed Music City. Major record labels, the Grand Ole Opry, and the Country Music Hall of Fame are all located in Nashville.

Fact file
The Grand Ole Opry country music radio program based in Nashville, Tennessee, started on November 28, 1925, and is the oldest radio program running in the United States

◄ Music in the streets of the French Quarter is a year-round tradition in New Orleans.

Dance

Several styles of dance have their roots in the Southeast. Tap dancing grew out of the African and Caribbean background of slaves. It was very popular from the late 1800s until the late 1900s. Lately, modern salsa dancers have made the style popular again.

Clogging is a traditional style of dance from the Appalachian Mountains. It combines dance forms from the United Kingdom, France, and Germany. Unlike tap dancers, who move their entire bodies, cloggers remain in one basic position and perform movements called steps with their feet.

Salsa!

In Spanish, *salsa* means "sauce." But since the 1960s, this word has also meant a style of music and dance with roots in Africa and the Caribbean countries of Puerto Rico and Cuba. At first, salsa was mostly popular with Cuban and Puerto Rican immigrants. But stars such as Gloria Estefan made it popular with other audiences.

◄ Salsa music and dance is popular at carnivals that take place in the Southeast.

Creole and Cajun cuisine

Two styles of cooking grew out of the mix of cultures in Louisiana. Both styles of cooking still use the types of meat, seafood, crops, and spices that early settlers used. But *Creole* cooking, which began with wealthy planters, refers to local foods prepared in a classical European style. *Cajun* cooking, on the other hand, usually means a one-pot meal that combines vegetables, spices, rice, and wild game or seafood.

Food

Bring your appetite when you visit the Southeast! The region is famous for its southern cooking. Fried chicken, corn bread, biscuits, grits, sweet potato pie—all are traditional foods from this region. This type of cuisine is often called soul food. Southerners and visitors alike enjoy these dishes.

After a meal of boiled, spiced crawfish, your hands will be red and you'll need a big glass of water to cool down the spicy taste!

Low country cuisine

Coastal South Carolina and Georgia are known as the low country. People of Caribbean descent who settled the islands there developed their own language, culture, and cooking style called Gullah. A "low country boil" is a traditional meal of shrimp cooked with grits.

Cuban food

Cuban food has become popular in parts of the Southeast, especially in south Florida, where Cuban immigrants began arriving in the late 1950s. Many dishes, such as black beans and rice, are flavored with green peppers, onions, garlic, oregano, and black pepper.

Grits

Grits are made from corn that has been dried and then stripped from the cob. When the kernels are soaked in liquid that contains lime or wood ash, they swell. The resulting food is called hominy. Grits are dried, ground hominy. Grits are such a southern tradition that grit is a nickname for someone who was born and raised in the South.

◄ A Southern-fried meal includes food cooked in hot fat as well as foods such as pecan pie and mashed potato.

Sports

The Kentucky Derby is the biggest horse race in the Southeast and one of the most famous races in the world. It takes place at Churchill Downs in Louisville, Kentucky, on the first Saturday in May every year.

Outdoor sports

Mild, warm weather during much of the year means that outdoor sports are popular. Golf courses, such as Augusta in Georgia and Pinehurst in North Carolina, bring visitors from around the world. Since the 1970s bicycle racing has been one of the region's popular outdoor sports.

Tiger Woods won the Professional Golfers' Association Masters Tournament at Pinehurst, North Carolina, in 2005.

About twenty horses compete in the 1.25-mile (2-kilometer) Kentucky Derby race.

Water sports

With so much coastline, it's no wonder that many sports in the Southeast involve water. Surfing, snorkeling, fishing, water-skiing, scuba diving, sailing, and swimming are all popular regional activities. In southern Florida, it's possible to do these activities year-round.

College sports

While the number of professional sports teams is growing, fans still focus on college games in the Southeast. Tickets to games at big schools, such as the University of Georgia, the University of Alabama, the University of North Carolina, Duke, Wake Forest, and Vanderbilt, are in high demand. Many famous professional players, such as Michael Jordan, started out on college teams in the Southeast.

There is a strong rivalry between basketball fans of Duke University in Durham, North Carolina, and the University of North Carolina at Chapel Hill.

Tractor pulls

At fairs and arenas around the region, tractor pulls are a popular sport. A tractor pull is an event in which souped-up tractors try to pull a weight, called a sled, for a distance of between 100 and 300 feet (30 and 90 meters). The tractor that tows the weight the farthest wins.

Hiking and camping

There are many state and national parks in the Southeast. Among them is the most visited in the United States—the Great Smoky Mountains National Park on the border between Tennessee and North Carolina. The park has more than 800 miles (1,287 kilometers) of trails, 70 miles (113 kilometers) of which are part of the Appalachian Trail. Visitors can hike or ride horses through miles of wilderness.

Appalachian Trail

One of the most famous outdoor attractions in the Southeast is the Appalachian Trail, which stretches more than 2,000 miles (3,218 kilometers) from Georgia to Maine. More than 400 miles (644 kilometers) of the trail cross through Georgia, North Carolina, and Tennessee.

Green Briar Creek runs through Smoky Mountains National Park. ▼

Living in the past

The rich history of the Southeast has left its mark on the land and the people of the region. One popular activity is **reenactment**. Reenactors study a certain time period and in some cases study specific events or battles. In their spare time they reenact, or play out, daily life or important events for visitors to see.

Reenactors help visitors learn about life in the past. ▼

Scenic drives

Some scenic drives are part of the national park system. The Natchez Trace Parkway, which stretches from Natchez, Mississippi, to Nashville, Tennessee, was built on the route of a trail used as early as 1733 by French traders. The Blue Ridge Parkway crosses from North Carolina into Virginia. As many as 20 million tourists visit this 469-mile (755-kilometer) drive each year.

The cat versus the buffalo

The annual World Catfish Festival in Belzoni, Mississippi, celebrates the importance of catfish in the Mississippi Delta. A parade, food, music, and crafts round out the day. People who work in catfish production plants started their own celebration—the buffalo fish festival. The buffalo is a Mississippi freshwater fish that can be eaten instead of catfish. This festival focuses attention on the poor working conditions in catfish production plants.

Festivals and holidays

One of the biggest celebrations in the Southeast is Mardi Gras. The event comes from a custom for a feast that French Catholics brought to New Orleans. This feast grew into a big celebration. Today, Mardi Gras in New Orleans is a month-long celebration that includes concerts, parades, and parties.

People dressed in costumes travel on floats and give away beads during the annual Mardi Gras parade in New Orleans.
▼

Martin Luther King Jr. holiday

Martin Luther King Jr. won the **Nobel Peace Prize** in 1964 for his leadership in the struggle against **racial discrimination**, much of which took place in Southeastern cities. Today, on Martin Luther King Jr. Day in January, church services, speeches, and music across the Southeast honor the memory of Dr. King.

Pig pickin'

In some parts of the country, barbecue means hamburgers, steaks, or hot dogs cooked on the grill. In other places it means ribs covered in thick, dark sauce and cooked over an open flame. In the Southeast it means a party featuring pork brushed with a thin sauce of vinegar and peppers, then cooked on a special grill that imitates an old-fashioned barbecue pit, then pulled from the bone and served on a paper plate with coleslaw. A "pig pickin'" is a traditional way to celebrate an important occasion, such as a birthday or anniversary.

Hollerin'

If people are always telling you to quiet down, you might want to take a trip to Spiveys Corner, North Carolina. Each year, the National Hollerin' Contest takes place there on the third Saturday in June. Hollerin' was a way for mountain dwellers and farmers to communicate with each other or to call animals across great distances. The event features contests for men, women, and children.

These women are dressed for a Caribbean celebration in Miami, Florida.

An Amazing Region

Under the ground

Some of the Southeast's most interesting places are underground. Hot mineral springs bubble from the ground in the mountainous parts of Arkansas, Georgia, North Carolina, and Tennessee. Northern and central Florida are dotted with **sinkholes**, formed by water wearing away beds of limestone. This part of the state was once known for its clear, cold springs. This important source of freshwater, which supplies more than 10 million people, is in danger. As Florida's population grows, more and more water is being pumped from below ground, emptying the springs.

The rich cultural heritage and history of the Southeast means that this region of the country has its own customs, music, types of food, and celebrations. The sounds of bluegrass, delta blues, piedmont blues, jazz, salsa, and rock 'n roll are typical of the Southeast. In fact, most of America's music was born in the Southeast.

Southern hospitality means that all are welcome to try the Southeast's cuisine, culture, music, and traditions. Many people visit the region, such as Northerners escaping the cold winter months. In fact the Southeast has some of the most popular tourist destinations in the United States.

The Kentucky bluegrass region is famous for its champion racehorses, shown grazing at dawn in a misty field.

Southern attractions

People are attracted to the Southeast for its warm climate and landforms. There is something for everyone in the landforms of the Southeast, which include beaches, bayous, and colorful mountains. There are also acres of forests and miles of hiking trails to explore.

Just one visit and many people do not ever want to leave. Friendly people, beautiful scenery, a rich history and culture, warm weather, and good food all help to make the Southeast one of the fastest-growing regions in the United States.

Hanging Rock State Park is one of more than 30 state parks in North Carolina. ▶

Visitors can paddle through crystal-clear, spring-fed rivers, salt marshes, or the murky waters of an eerie bayou in the Southeast. ▼

NASCAR

The noise is deafening. Colorful cars zoom around the track as the checkered flag snaps in the breeze. They weave boldly in and out, coming so close to one another that they almost touch. This is a National Association for Stock Cars Auto Racing (NASCAR) event in Talladega, Alabama. NASCAR races are competitions between cars on a steeply sloped oval track. Speeds during races can reach up to 190 miles (300 kilometers) per hour. The first official NASCAR race was held in North Carolina in June, 1949.

51

Find Out More

World Wide Web

The Fifty States

www.infoplease.com/states.html

This website has a clickable U.S. map that gives facts about each of the 50 states, plus images of each state's flag.

These sites have pictures, statistics, and other facts about each state in the Southeast:

Alabama
www.state.al.us

Arkansas
www.arkansas.com

Florida
www.myflorida.com

Georgia
www.georgia.org/tourism

Kentucky
www.kytourism.com

Louisiana
www.crt.state.la.us

Mississippi
www.visitmississippi.org

North Carolina
www.visitnc.com

South Carolina
www.discoversouthcarolina.com

Tennessee
www.state.tn.us

Books to read

Johnson, Michael. *Native Tribes of the Southeast.* Milwaukee: World Almanac Library, 2004.

National Geographic Society. *The Southeast Today.* Washington, DC: National Geographic Society, 2004.

Rikson, Pauline. *Daily Life on a Southern Plantation–1853.* Collingdale, PA: Diane Publishing Co., 2004.

Places to visit

Biltmore Estate (Asheville, North Carolina)
   Tour a mansion with more than 150 rooms!

Coca-Cola Museum (Atlanta, Georgia)
   This museum tells the story of the famous soft drink.

Great Smoky Mountains National Park (Tennessee and North Carolina)
   This is the most visited national park in the United States.

John C. Campbell Folk School (Brasstown, North Carolina)
   Appalachian culture comes alive at this school, which offers lessons in arts, crafts, and music.

Historic St. Augustine (St. Augustine, Florida)
   The country's oldest city offers tours and other attractions.

International Motorsports Hall of Fame and Museum (Talladega, Alabama)
   A collection of vehicles are on show at this museum.

Sun Studio (Memphis, Tennessee)
   This recording studio is considered to be the birth place of rock-and-roll.

Timeline

before 1492
Many Native American cultures thrive all across the Southeast.

1492
Christopher Columbus discovers the New World.

1513
Juan Ponce de León comes ashore near what is now St. Augustine and names the area Florida.

1565
The Spanish build a fort at St. Augustine, Florida.

1587
The Lost Colony is established on the coast of present-day North Carolina.

1682
Robert LaSalle claims the entire Mississippi Valley for France and calls it Louisiana.

1699
France makes Louisiana a colony.

1720
The French establish New Orleans as the capital of Louisiana.

1733
The city of Savannah, Georgia, is founded.

1763
The British win the French and Indian War, forcing France to give them land east of the Mississippi River; land west of the Mississippi goes to Spain.

1775
The Revolutionary War begins; Daniel Boone blazes a trail through the Cumberland Gap and establishes Boonesboro in present-day Tennessee.

1783
The Revolutionary War ends.

1800
Spain returns Louisiana to France.

1803
France sells Louisiana to the United States for $15 million.

1812
The United States fights Great Britain in the War of 1812 until 1815.

1838
U.S. government troops force Cherokees to leave their lands in Georgia, North Carolina, and Tennessee and walk to Oklahoma along the Trail of Tears.

1860
Abraham Lincoln is elected president of the United States; South Carolina leaves the Union over the issue of slavery.

1861
Georgia, Florida, Mississippi, Arkansas, North Carolina, Alabama, Tennessee, and Louisiana also leave the Union; the Civil War begins.

1864
Union general William T. Sherman burns Atlanta, Georgia, to the ground, then marches to Savannah to crush the Confederacy.

1865
The Civil War ends.

1866
Tennessee is the first Confederate state to rejoin the Union.

1870
Mississippi is the last Confederate state to rejoin the Union.

1875
The first Kentucky Derby is held in Louisville, Kentucky.

1964
President Lyndon Johnson signs the Civil Rights Act; Dr. Martin Luther King Jr. receives the Nobel Peace Prize.

1968
Dr. Martin Luther King Jr. is assassinated in Memphis, Tennessee.

1977
Georgia peanut farmer Jimmy Carter is elected president of the United States.

1992
Arkansas governor Bill Clinton becomes president of the United States; Tennessee senator Al Gore becomes vice president.

2005
Hurricane Katrina strikes the Gulf Coast, killing hundreds and destroying homes and businesses.

States at a Glance

Alabama
Became State: 1819
Nickname: The Heart of Dixie
Motto: *Audemus jura nostra defendera*—"We dare defend our rights"
Capital: Montgomery
Bird: Yellowhammer
Flower: Camellia

Arkansas
Became State: 1836
Nickname: The Natural State
Motto: *Regnat Populus*—"The people rule"
Capital: Little Rock
Bird: Mockingbird
Flower: Apple blossom

Georgia
Became State: 1788
Nickname: The Peach State
Motto: Wisdom, Justice, and Moderation
Capital: Atlanta
Bird: Brown thrasher
Flower: Azalea

Florida
Became State: 1845
Nickname: The Sunshine State
Motto: In God We Trust
Capital: Tallahassee
Bird: Mockingbird
Flower: Orange blossom

Kentucky
Became State: 1792
Nickname: The Bluegrass State
Motto: United we stand, divided we fall
Capital: Frankfort
Bird: Cardinal
Flower: Goldenrod

Louisiana
Became State: 1812
Nickname: The Magnolia State
Motto: Union, justice, and confidence
Capital: Baton Rouge
Bird: Mockingbird
Flower: Magnolia

Mississippi
Became State: 1817
Nickname: The Pelican State
Motto: *Virtute et armis*—"By valor and arms"
Capital: Jackson
Bird: Brown pelican
Flower: Magnolia

North Carolina
Became State: 1789
Nickname: The Old North State
Motto: *Esse quam videri*—"To be, rather than to seem"
Capital: Raleigh
Bird: Cardinal
Flower: Dogwood

South Carolina
Became State: 1788
Nickname: The Palmetto State
Motto: *Animis Opibusque Parati*—"Prepared in mind and resources" and *Dum Spiro Spero*—"While I breathe, I hope"
Capital: Columbia
Bird: Carolina wren
Flower: Yellow jessamine

Tennessee
Became State: 1796
Nickname: The Volunteer State
Motto: Agriculture and Commerce
Capital: Nashville
Bird: Mockingbird
Flower: Iris

Glossary

bayous marshy streams connected to a larger body of water

beach erosion gradual wearing away of beaches by waves and wind

cash crops crops grown to sell rather than for feed

climate weather conditions of a place

coastal plain flat, sandy land with few trees, located near an ocean or gulf

company towns towns built by factories or other businesses so that workers have a place to live

Confederate States of America government formed by the states of Alabama, Arkansas, Florida, Georgia, Louisiana, Mississippi, North Carolina, South Carolina, and Tennessee during the Civil War

Continental Army army that fought for independence during the Revolutionary War

delta area of land formed by sand and mud at the mouth of a river

descendants people who come from a specific group or background

Dixieland music style of jazz music from the early 1900s that started in New Orleans

economy system of money in a place

endangered threatened

hardwoods trees that have leaves and flowers, such as oak or maple trees

immigrants people who leave their country to settle in another

invasive plants plants that are not native to a particular place and that begin to take over other plants in an area

light rail rail transportation system that uses electric-powered rail cars along tracks used only for that purpose

Louisiana Purchase agreement signed in 1803 in which the United States bought France's land in North America

mainland main land mass of a country or area

mass transit transportation that is designed to move large numbers of people around a city

metropolitan word used to describe a large city

mint place where coins are made

Nobel Peace Prize prize named for a Swedish scientist, Alfred Nobel, and awarded each year to people who have worked for world peace

patriots people loyal to their country

pesticides chemicals used to kill insects

piedmont foothills

racial discrimination treating someone unfairly because of his or her skin color

reenactment study of a historical event, such as a battle, which is then repeated as accurately as possible

Revolutionary War war fought against Great Britain by the American colonies between 1775 and 1783

service industry work connected with the serving of customers

sharecroppers farmers who live on land they do not own and must give part of their crops to the landowner as rent

sinkholes lowering of the surface of the land due to an underground cavern or gap

subtropical having a climate similar to the very warm, humid places near the equator

sprawl spread out

swamps areas of low land that is often flooded

textiles cloth that is woven or knitted

tropical hot and humid

Union A name for the United States during the Civil War

wetlands low-lying lands with tall grasses but few or no trees

Index

Alabama, 6, 14, 16, 17, 19, 31, 32, 35, 39, 45, 51
animals, 15, 20, 21, 33, 36
Appalachian Mountains, 4, 16, 17, 28, 29, 31
Appalachian Trail, 5, 46
Arkansas, 5, 6, 10, 16, 17, 28, 31, 32, 36, 37, 50
Atlanta, Georgia, 7, 24
Atlantic Ocean, 14, 18, 19, 20, 27, 35

barrier islands, 14
bayous, 15, 21
birds, 20, 21
Blue Ridge Mountains, 17
Boone, Daniel, 16, 28

Cajun culture, 10, 42
Cape Canaveral, Florida, 39
Charlotte, North Carolina, 7, 25
Civil War, 12, 27
climate, 6, 18, 19, 22, 51
coastal plain, 14, 15, 16
Confederate States of America, 12
cotton, 13, 24, 32, 33

dance, 41
Deep South, 31

endangered species, 15, 20
European exploration, 9, 26, 27, 28
European settlers, 8, 9, 10, 11, 16, 28
Everglades National Park, 15

farming, 7, 13, 15, 22, 24, 30, 31, 32, 33, 36
fish, 21, 36, 48
Florida, 5, 6, 7, 14, 15, 20, 22, 25, 26, 27, 29, 32, 36, 38, 39, 43, 44, 50
foods, 42, 43, 49

Georgia, 5, 6, 7, 8, 10, 14, 16, 17, 18, 24, 27, 31, 32, 43, 44, 45, 46, 50
Grant, Ulysses S., 12
Great Depression, 24

Great Smoky Mountains, 17
Gulf of Mexico, 14, 18, 19, 20, 35, 39
Gullah culture, 43

Hines, Gregory, 41
Huntsville, Alabama, 39
hurricanes, 19, 39

immigrants, 8, 27, 43

Jacksonville, Florida, 7
Jordan, Michael, 45

Kentucky, 5, 6, 8, 12, 16, 17, 18, 28, 44
Kentucky Derby, 44
Kentucky Fried Chicken, 37
King, Martin Luther Jr., 49

Lee, Robert E., 12
Lincoln, Abraham, 12
Little Rock, Arkansas, 28
Louisiana, 5, 7, 10, 14, 15, 19, 32, 38
Louisiana Purchase, 10, 26
Louisville, Kentucky, 44

Mammoth Cave, 5, 17
manufacturing, 7, 25
Mardi Gras, 5, 6, 48
Memphis, Tennessee, 7, 28
Miami, Florida, 7, 27, 35
Mississippi, 6, 7, 10, 14, 15, 19, 26, 28, 31, 32, 35, 40, 47, 48
Mississippi Delta, 15, 21, 36, 48
Mississippi River, 10, 26, 28
music, 6, 28, 40, 41, 50

Nashville, Tennessee, 7, 40, 47
National Association for Stock Car Auto Racing (NASCAR), 51
national parks, 8, 15, 17, 46, 47
Native Americans, 8, 9, 27, 28
New Orleans, Louisiana, 5, 6, 19, 26, 35, 38, 40, 48
North Carolina, 5, 6, 7, 8, 9, 10, 11, 14, 16, 17, 18, 25, 32, 37, 38, 44, 45, 46, 47, 49, 50

Orlando, Florida, 7

piedmont, 16, 18, 23
plants, 15, 16, 18, 20, 21, 22, 23
Ponce de León, Juan, 26
population, 6, 7, 25, 27, 34, 50
Presley, Elvis, 28

racial discrimination, 49
Raleigh, Sir Walter, 9
reenactments, 47
Revolutionary War, 11, 12, 25
Roosevelt, Franklin D., 29

Savannah, Georgia, 5, 27
Sherman, William, 27
sinkholes, 50
slavery, 9, 12, 13, 41
South Carolina, 6, 7, 11, 12, 14, 16, 17, 32, 43
sports, 44, 45, 51
St. Augustine, Florida, 26, 38
St. Petersburg, Florida, 7
state parks, 46
Sunbelt, 6
swamps, 14, 15, 21

Tampa, Florida, 7
Tennessee, 5, 6, 7, 8, 10, 16, 17, 18, 25, 39, 40, 46, 47, 50
Tennessee-Tombigbee Waterway, 35
textile industry, 13, 36
tobacco, 15, 24, 32, 33, 36
tourism, 5, 6, 26, 38, 47, 50
transportation, 30, 32, 33, 34, 35, 36
trees, 16, 18, 20, 21, 22, 23

universities, 38, 45

Vanderbilt, George, 29
Virginia, 11, 12, 47

Warm Springs, Georgia, 29
wetlands, 14, 21
Winston-Salem, North Carolina, 37